KERALA

RAGHUBIR SINGH

KERALA

The Spice Coast of India

with 87 colour photographs
including 3 panoramics

THAMES AND HUDSON

For Devika

First published in Great Britain in 1986 by Thames and Hudson Ltd, London

Photographs copyright © 1986 by Raghubir Singh
Introduction copyright © 1986 by Raghubir Singh
Photographic layout by Raghubir Singh

Printed in Switzerland. Bound in France.

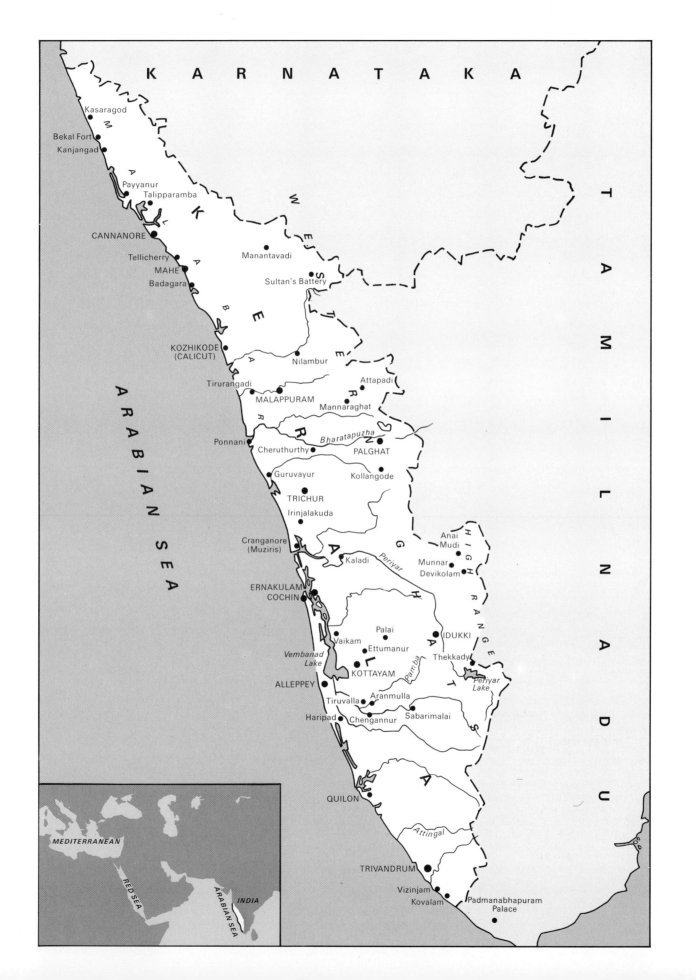

Acknowledgments

I would like to offer my deepest thanks to Mammen and Prema Mathew, T. C. Satyanath, Appan and Kamla Menon, Thomas and Simi Vallikappen, Jaiprakash Paliath, Dr P. R. G. Mathur, Kavalam Narayan Pannicker, Rajan and Hira Narayan, Michael A. Kallibayallil, Hashim Kaderkutty, Len and Dawn Latham and C. P. Radhakrishnan, who opened their homes and offices to me and provided invaluable advice. I would also like to acknowledge my gratitude to K. Aboobacker, Sasi Booshan, William Gedney, Adoor Gopalakrishnan, P. Gopi, Ramakrishnan Kadamanitta, Umar Koya, Valsala Kumari, Murkot Kunhappa, Dr K. N. Kurup, Princess Gauri, M. C. Namboodiripad, O. M. C. Namboodiripad, Olappamanna Subramanyam Namboodiripad, P. M. Raman Namboodiripad, T. Narayanan, Gopal Menon, Ramesh Menon, K. M. Mathew, Jacob Mathew, Phillip Mathew, Dr K. N. Raj, Trichur P. Radhakrishnan, H. Y. Sharada Prasad, G. Venu and N. Vishwanathan Nair.

Finally, I must thank my wife for her patience and understanding during the long periods of travel the book required, in the last four years, and also for her excellent translation into French, in spite of my constant revisions and changes of the English text, which made her task very difficult.

Introduction

In North India, our heritage evolved from the waves of migrants who entered the Indian Plain through the northern passes, from Aryan times to Moghul times. My own direct ancestors used the same passes in the 7th century and eventually settled in Rajasthan – a desert land dotted with forts and enriched by a tradition of martial heroes, medieval chivalry and stirring battles. Growing up in this land of rousing history, the only other places which held me captive were the Himalayas and the Ganges, because our religious life and literature were deeply rooted in them.

As a child I had little reason to look towards the tip of India. When my mother read from the Ramayana, the revered Hindu epic, I learned about Lanka, the island in the south, where the demon Ravana dwelt. The seas of the south seemed far away and sinister and South India itself was a land of darkness, inhabited by dark-skinned people.

In the summer, the hot and dusty wind, the *loo*, would obscure the fort under whose shadows we lived. One day, when the monsoon had brought relief and my school reopened, my geography teacher said, 'Boys, I have made a geographer's pilgrimage to Kerala during these last holidays. There, I have seen the south-west monsoon build up over the Arabian Sea and strike the windward slopes of the Western Ghats, giving India its first rains.' Then, pausing to shift the betel-nut in his mouth, he continued, 'Those rain clouds have taken over a month to reach Rajasthan.'

In my school, only a few students were South Indians, and they were not in my class. They were quiet and kept to themselves. I first made friends with a Malayali (one who speaks Malayalam, the language of Kerala) when I attended college in New Delhi. Appan Menon was my neighbour in the college hostel. I remember him once chiding me, 'You feudal fellow, if you ever go to Kerala you will learn what democracy is all about.'

Kerala was formed in 1956 by the merging of three Malayalam-speaking areas – Malabar in Madras state and the former princely provinces of Travancore and Cochin. I first went there in 1967 for the *New York Times Magazine*. Elamkulam Mana Sankaran Namboodiripad had just become Chief Minister, after a Communist-dominated coalition had romped to power in the state's legislative elections. Ten years earlier, Kerala's Communist Party under E.M.S. (as he is popularly called) had stunned the world by scoring the first major success for Communism in a democratic country.* This had led the American press to brand Kerala as the Yennan of India. My second visit, in 1970, was to illustrate an article in the *New York Times* on Kerala's matrilineal system, which was published on the American Mother's Day.

Before I went to Kerala the first time, I had travelled widely in North India, which was in the throes of famine. I had grown accustomed not only to the ubiquitous arid expanse of my native Rajasthan, but also to the parched and scrubby land of the Gangetic Plain. Therefore Kerala's lovely lagoons, its beguiling backwaters, its many rivers, its land coloured like a parrot's back, its characteristic coconut trees buffeted by the sea breeze, and the sight and sound of the waves captured my imagination. I also noted that there was no starvation in Kerala, as there was in the north, though it has a population of 25 million. On the 1970 visit I learned a Malayali saying: 'The God who made Kerala had a green thumb.'

In 1982 I stood on Sankaracharya Hill in Kashmir. My work in the vale** was over and I looked south to the other end of India. I wanted a complete change, and the Malabar*** Coast, as Kerala is also known, instantly came to mind. That same year I booked a passage to Kerala.

* After the tiny Italian principality of San Marino.
** Raghubir Singh, *Kashmir, Garden of the Himalayas*, London, New York, Bombay, Hong Kong, 1983.
*** Malabar covers northern Kerala from Trichur to Kasargode, while the Malabar Coast is a term denoting the whole state of Kerala.

The Heartland

Once there, I planned my travels by scanning a map of the central part of the state. I ran my eyes over Cranganore, Kaladi, Cheruthurthy and Guruvayur. They are the four corners and landmarks of Kerala's heartland. In the centre of this territory lies the important temple-town of Trichur. For Malayalis this tract bounded by two rivers, the sacred Bharatapuzha and the Periyar, has a special meaning. It once looked out to the maritime world and it has a deep-rooted cultural tradition of saints, poets, writers and performing artists.

I began my tour of Kerala's heartland at Cranganore, in ancient times Muziris, near the point where the Periyar flows into the sea. Under the coconut trees whipped by the wind the fishing boats were parked upside down. Thirty yards behind them stood a few tile-roofed huts. In their shade six sunburnt men were meticulously mending nets. This lonely shore could have been any unknown stretch on the 590 kilometre coastline of Kerala. In this enchanted place, I could have found a peaceful lodging for a peppercorn rent.

Maritime Spice Trade

Yet, at one time, this was a rich port. What Bombay and Calcutta are to our times, Muziris was to ancient India. And even more. It was a fabled place. An early Tamil* poet, from neighbouring Tamilnadu, chanted its praise: 'The thriving town of Muchiri, where the beautiful great ships of the Yavanas [Greeks], bringing gold, come splashing the white foam on the waters of the Periyar . . . and return laden with pepper.' Phoenicians, Egyptians, Persians, Chinese, Romans and Arabs were other callers at this spice emporium.

* Malayalam, the language of Kerala, originated as a Tamil dialect. In its development it incorporated a deep Sanskrit base and infusions of language from foreign traders and settlers.

The earliest mention of Muziris is in the first century AD, when an anonymous Alexandrian mariner wrote *Periplus Maris Erythroei or Circumnavigating the Indian Ocean*. He mentions that the exports from Puteoli, the Roman commercial port, to Muziris were flowered robes, eye-pigment, chrysolite, white glass (probably mica), copper or brass, tin, lead and some wine. The Roman imports from Muziris, besides spices, were also, curiously enough, Malabar monkeys, tigers, parrots and elephants accompanied by their mahouts.

But the demand for spices in Rome was so great and the price of pepper (*Karuthu Ponnu* or black-gold as it is still called in Kerala) so high as to cause an economic drain. Roman products alone could not pay for the pepper required. Pliny the Elder (AD 23-79) complained in his *Natural History*: 'It is surprising that the use of pepper has come so much into fashion. Commodities as a rule attract us by their appearance or utility, but the only quality of pepper is its pungency, and yet it is for this very undesirable element that we import it in very huge quantities . . .[from] the first emporium of India, Muziris . . .'

Hoards of Roman gold coins have been discovered in Kerala. Today antique dealers in Trivandrum, the capital city, sell them illegally to tourists for up to Rs.15,000.00 ($1,200.00). The coins date from the time of the Emperors Nero, Hadrian, Tiberius and Trajan (AD 14-138). When Alaric the Goth besieged Rome in 408, he raised the siege for 3,000 pounds of pepper.

Three factors boosted the booming trade. First, the Phoenician, Greek and Etruscan advances in the science of shipbuilding led to merchant ships that were broad and heavy with plenty of space for storage. Aristotle likened them to large insects with small, weak wings trying to fly. Second, in about AD 50 the Greek merchant-mariner Hippalus learned from the Arabs of the monsoon winds, especially their force and their frequency. Third, the habits of the mysterious Malabar mud-banks were discovered.

The effluent from the Periyar and other rivers contains a high suspension of laterite, a brick-like substance. This yields an unctuous and semi-liquid mud which, when carried out to the sea, settles down offshore. When the south-west monsoon bursts, this tenacious stuff is stirred up to form a mud-bank, with a high rate of viscosity. Dispersed below the surface of the sea, this stratum of fluid-mud has the effect of tranquillizing the surf, almost like a barrier. The rougher the seas on the outer side of the mud-bank, the calmer the surf on the inner side – thus providing safe anchorage to ships.

The Arabs used the mud-banks and the monsoon winds particularly well. After the decline of Rome, when the Venetian merchant princes entered the spice trade, the Arabs, Turks and others acted as intermediaries between Malabar and the City of St Mark. The journey between Italy and the Malabar Coast, from the Mediterranean through the Red Sea or the Persian Gulf, took sixteen weeks.

On the trade route from China to Rome, Muziris and the port of Quilon in southern Kerala were important stations. Jars, pans and parasols are still known in Kerala as *China Bharani*, *China Chatti* and *China kkuda*. Chinese fishing nets dot the coast and the state's considerable fireworks production is a Chinese legacy.

Muziris was the capital of the Cheras or Keralas from the second to the eighth century AD. As their kingdom thrived on sea trade, its inhabitants warmly welcomed foreign traders and were friendly towards strangers. The great religions also used the maritime trade routes to find a footing and a safe haven in Kerala. The Apostle St Thomas is believed to have brought Christianity to India in AD 52 through Muziris. The Jews* sought shelter there, most likely in AD 70, after the destruction of the second Jerusalem Temple, and the diaspora that followed that event. Other Jews came later, from

* Nowadays about 30 White Jews are left in Kerala, mainly in Cochin. There were about 2,000 in 1947. The Black Jews (Myuchasims), probably descendants of the early settlers who intermarried, are not to be found in Kerala. Bombay is the home of 6,000 Jews out of the total Indian Jewish population of about 7,000. Large numbers of Indian Jews have migrated to Israel.

Portuguese to British times. However, their legends speak of the ships of King Solomon (972-932 BC) trading with the Malabar Coast. And a deep-rooted Malabar tradition holds that the last Cheraman Perumal, the king of Muziris, embraced Islam, made the pilgrimage to Medina and met the Prophet, though he died on the return voyage.

But the glory of Muziris was not to last. The Portuguese built a fort there in 1523 and considered using it as their base; instead, they chose to develop Cochin, for the mysterious Malabar mud-banks had moved inshore and choked the mouth of the Periyar. Cochin's natural harbour, which had not existed in the first century AD, was now fully formed and ready to become a port. Calicut was already a rival port and Quilon had been active for a long time, especially with the Chinese trade. Muziris, today known as Cranganore, is a village several miles from the seafront. St Thomas is remembered there with a modern monument; the Muslims have rebuilt their original mosque; and the Bhadrakali temple, Kerala's most important Hindu shrine to the Mother Goddess who guards her shores, stands nearby. As for the Perumals – the tolerant trading kings – a pathetic contemporary pillar with a plaque, beside a soccer ground, is their sole monument.

Kaladi and Sankaracharya

While the rulers of Muziris were enriched by the traffic of the maritime trade routes, there was one Keralite who used the inland trade routes which criss-crossed ancient India to perform a personal odyssey and leave an indelible imprint on India's religious philosophy and culture. In spite of his influence, little is known about Sankaracharya's birth and life. There is a school of thought which maintains that between 44 BC and 800 AD there lived not one, but many, Sankaracharyas, and that only this fact can explain the prodigious legend. But the popular belief is that there was only one, born into a

Brahmin family at Kaladi, on the Periyar, directly east of Cranganore. Sankaracharya died at the age of only 32. In his short life he emphasized the illusory nature of the world and preached that reality lies beyond the bounds of normal human senses and that only asceticism, through disciplined control of the senses, can allow a glimpse of its true nature. His doctrine of monism is called Advaita Vedanta.

Sankaracharya vigorously propagated this philosophy through an epic of travel, from the lower tip of India to Tibet. He is credited with the dramatic resurgence of Hinduism and the decline of Buddhism – which was a popular religion in India, including Kerala, until the eighth century. He is also presumed to have played a prominent role in pulling Hinduism out of the rut of ritualism and the chaos of sectarian interpretations of its philosophy. In effect, he rehauled the entire fabric of Hinduism by adopting some of Buddhism's own philosophy and organization, to the extent that he has been called a crypto-Buddhist. The Hinduism which evolved from the Sankaracharya tradition is carried on by colleges he established at Sringeri in the South, Badri in the Himalayas, and Dwarka and Puri on the western and eastern seaboards respectively. The colleges' pontiff-like heads, called Sankaracharyas, are the voices of Hinduism. In this way the enigmatic Sankaracharya legend, from ancient to modern times, has bound disparate India in the knot of the Hindu religion.

Cheruthurthy and the Kathakali Theatre

From Kaladi, the lovely birthplace of Sankaracharya, to Cheruthurthy is a three-hour drive through groves of coconuts, between paddy fields and across meandering rivers. The Kalamandalam, the best known school of Kerala's performing arts, is situated there by the banks of the Bharatapuzha. The poet Vallathol Narayana Menon founded the school in 1930 in his native village and it is a memorial to his passion for the performing arts, notably for Kerala's extraordinary art of Kathakali.

Kathakali (literally, story-play) combines elements of pantomime, passion plays, opera, ballet and costume dance-drama. It was developed in the sixteenth century by the Raja of Kottarakara, in southern Kerala.

I arrived at Kalamandalam one day before dawn, during the monsoon, and heard the drums summoning students to class. The students undergo vigorous training in this season. In high-roofed sheds, boys between 12 and 20, wearing loin-cloths, dripped with sweat and shone from the rubbing of oil. Some of them stood by waiting their turn and others lay on coir mats while a guru holding on to a bar used his feet to massage them from head to toe. For several hours this rigorous routine continued. One student explained: 'First the massage is painful, but soon it relaxes us. Then we begin to enjoy it. It loosens up our bodies.'

In the strenuous six-year course the students learn to use the eyes for expression and the fingers and body movements for subtle and precise gestures and suggestions. When the Kathakali training is finished, the performers must be able to convey the nine emotions of love, valour, pathos, wonder, derision, disgust, fear, fury and serenity, as well as the twenty-four basic *mudras* or gestures, which can substitute for speech when combined and lucidly executed.

During a Kathakali performance the on-stage orchestra is composed of the 30-pound vertical drums called *chendas*, struck with short sticks; the even heavier horizontal drums, the *maddalams*, tapped with the fingers; tiny cymbals; a gong; and a harmonium. Two singers chant the story in a mixture of Sanskrit and Malayalam.

Since nothing like Kathakali exists elsewhere in India or abroad, it is Kerala's most widely exported art. But when it was chosen to open the inaugural Washington, D.C., ceremony of the Festival of India which took place in the US in 1985, it put many Westerners to sleep, even though the performance was short. The diplomats, bureaucrats and politicians were not accustomed to its slow tempo.

Kathakali takes you into a world of deities, demons, heroes, heroines, sages, soldiers and satyrs. Over 2,000 performances, many of them lasting all night, are held annually in Kerala. The stories are taken from the Indian epics and other classics, especially the *Mahabharata*. The audiences know all of them by heart.

The Kalamandalam school maintains its own Kathakali troupe which performs all over India and sometimes abroad, as at the Washington opening. Both students and gurus participate. Kalamandalam is also a title given to an honoured student. The noted actor, Kalamandalam Krishnan Nair, was one of the early students of the school.

I have seen Krishnan Nair act many times. But for me his most memorable performance was his portrayal of Bhima, one of the five Pandava brothers, in *Duryodhana Vadham*. The audience seated on mats watched the two most important events of the *Mahabharata*: the banishment of the Pandavas after their defeat by their wicked cousins, the Kauravas, in a game of dice; and the ultimate triumph of the Pandavas over the Kauravas on the battlefield. In the dice game the eldest Pandava gambled away everything: his fortune, his fighting forces, his palace, his kingdom, his brothers, their shared wife Draupadi and even himself. Then the eldest Kaurava, Duryodhana, commanded his younger brother, Dussassana, to disrobe Draupadi in court. But the latter failed, for Draupadi appealed to Krishna, who caused her sari to unwind endlessly. Another game was played and again the Pandavas lost everything and were sent into exile for thirteen years. At the end of this time the Kauravas refused to return the kingdom and a war was fought. There, on the battlefield, Bhima fulfilled a vow over the insult to Draupadi. After a fierce fight he felled Dussassana and drank his blood.

In the dramatic moments of the fight and the killing, as naked feet pounded the wooden floor and the beat of the *chenda* rose to a climax, the sound washed through the palm-matted walls and floated over the paddy fields where first light was heralding a new tropical day. Farmers, on their way to harvest paddy, peeped in. Mothers roused their children from sleep to witness the triumph of good over evil after a long night's passage over many shades of human frailty. The play was almost at an end when a dishevelled Draupadi entered, bent down, and soaked her tangled hair in the blood of Dussassana. Then, realizing that in his rage he had become like an animal, Bhima fell at the feet of Krishna, who blessed his guilt away. Transformed into a cheerful human being, Krishnan Nair quit the stage.

Guruvayur: Sree Krishna Temple

My fourth stop on this round of Kerala's cultural heartland is Guruvayur. The town's nationwide fame is owed to its Sree Krishna temple, one of India's most popular temples, known for the fervent belief of its worshippers. This temple's history of casteism and orthodoxy made it unappealing to me. But I did find the offerings of its devotees most interesting. They offer their own weight in gold, silver, precious stones, sugar, butter, tender coconuts, bananas, coins, firewood, knives, coir and even brooms. This worship is termed *thulabharam*.* Later, the items are auctioned. One of the more unusual *thulabharams* was by a Malayali film-maker: for the weight of the footage of a feature film about to be premiered, he offered to the Lord of Guruvayur an equivalent weight in coconuts. And perhaps taking a cue from the film-maker, the local Marxist party participated in a similarly unorthodox *thulabharam*. When a Communist devotee of the Lord of Guruvayur offered a *thulabharam* of commodities weighing the same as a metal casting of the hammer, sickle and star – the emblem of Kerala's Marxists – the local party cell bought

* P. Venugopal, *Indian Express*, Cochin, 1 June 1984.

the metal casting from the temple and displayed it in their office. Perhaps Krishna blessed away any trace of religiosity in this Marxist symbol, just as he had blessed away the guilt of Bhima in the Kathakali play.

Trichur: Koodiyattam and the Pooram Festival

Unlike Guruvayur, Trichur, the nucleus of the heartland, is a temple-town I do like. The Vadukkanathan or Siva Temple complex stands in the middle of grounds bordered by a road which is alive with the roar of trucks and buses, the putter of three-wheeled taxis and the honking of a variety of horns. These sharp and screeching noises drown the occasional soft and muted sounds of an elephant loping by, its mahout riding eye-level with the shop signs. Shops, hotels, restaurants, coffee houses, banks and commercial establishments line the outer sides of the road. Thus the sacred heart of the city, sometimes called the second Kailas – after Hinduism and Buddhism's most sacred mountain – is surrounded by a blitz of brassy profanity. But the grounds of the temple are large enough to keep commerce at bay and, inside, the high walls shut out most of the sound and tranquillity reigns. One shrine at the Vadukkanathan contains early eighteenth-century murals which depict the story of the *Mahabharata*.

But the most striking of this complex of buildings is the Koothambalam, the temple theatre – the finest of its kind. It has an immense, steep copper roof with three elaborate finials. Inside and below the finials is the square stage with lacquered pillars and its own small roof. Here, seated on the wooden floor, I had the good fortune to watch 69-year-old Ammanur Madhav Chakyyar and his troupe perform Koodiyattam, the highly stylized theatrical art out of which Kathakali evolved, which incorporates dance, dramatics and mime. When I had previously watched Ammanur, the best Koodiyattam practitioner, perform in New Delhi on a Western stage, I was too far back in the large auditorium to appreciate his subtle art. But in the Trichur Koothambalam I could follow each gesture or expression. I was captivated. The Koodiyattam and Koothu* are traditionally performed by Chakyyars and only in temples, though now Koodiyattam is being taught at the Kalamandalam in Cheruthurthy.

Through stylistic gestures, Ammanur Madhar Chakyyar told the Ramayana story of Ravana kidnapping Sita. He evoked Ravana's troubled thoughts, emotions, moods and his maverick mind; and through pantomime he portrayed plants, flowers, birds and bees, forests, cities, palaces, and kings and queens. No painted backdrops were needed, only his expressive eyes and the delicate movement of his fingers seen by the light of a single bell-metal oil lamp with three wicks. This was an ancient technique approximating to the modern cinematic close-up. The occasional speech of the Chakyyar and the voice of the woman singer were loud and clear. There was also the measured play of a pipe, the thump of a copper drum, the clash of cymbals, the drone of a horn and the sonorous sound of a conch-shell. (The copper drum, the *mizhavu*, is a unique instrument. It is treated throughout its life like a Brahmin and when it is worn out it is buried with elaborate ritual.) The clarity of sound of the instruments made me look up to the heavy ornamental rafters, the railings, the wood-carvings, the columns and the covered stage under the copper roof. The architecture combined aesthetic decoration with superb acoustics. The Koothambalam is a perfect setting for a thousand-year-old tradition of classical theatre. No wonder that when Koodiyattam moves out of its old and ideal setting it loses much of its magic.

More than for its theatre, Trichur is known nationally for the yearly Pooram festival, which includes the spectacle of thirty caparisoned and parading elephants equally divided

---

* Koothu is a comic art which often comments on contemporary life and ridicules follies and foibles through a solo act of mime and facial expression. The performer also narrates classical and epic stories. It closely follows the principles laid down in the *Natya Shastra*, the ancient Sanskrit treatise on dance and theatre. Kathakali borrowed much from Koothu and Koodiyattam.

among two rival groups, who hold an ornamental parasol competition on elephant-back. There are also rows of musicians, torchlight processions, fireworks and, of course, large crowds. The setting is the Trichur grounds.

What is stunning during the Trichur Pooram – and outdoes even the Kandy Perahera, the biggest Buddhist festival of Sri Lanka – is the music, of which there are two kinds. In the *Panchavadayam*, the rolling beat of the *thimala* drum sets the pace for two other drums – the *maddalam* and *edakka* – and for the semicircular horns, the *kombu*; while the *ilathalam* or cymbals mark time. Soft, slow beats rise at the end to a complex and majestic climax, as if the gods had given the sound of the crashing Kerala sea a staccato rhythmic resonance. Even more thunderous is the *melam*, in which dozens of drummers, cymbalists and horn blowers join in energetic unison. The throngs of listeners flail the hot and humid pre-monsoon air with a sea of arms moving in time to the music. As the *melam* peaks, men rise up from the backs of elephants to wave whisks of white yak tails above the swaying crowd.

Standing in the middle of the packed Trichur temple compound in the fierce mid-May sun, I decided that the music was for the ear of the monsoon-god. And, indeed, Indra, God of rain and thunder, did reply within a fortnight with his own music – the pattering and pounding of rain on the Malabar Coast.

The Monsoon and the Onam Festival

To see the south-west monsoon arrive, I booked myself into a hotel room at Kovalam beach, near Trivandrum, Kerala's capital city. Daily the clouds advanced and retreated, their thunder like the sound of trumpeting elephants. Every day I scanned the newspapers for the countdown, given first in days, then in hours. Finally, the front page announced: 'The monsoon will break in 24 hours.' It hit Kovalam with force in the afternoon, after the sky had turned lead-grey. Fierce rain swept the coast and the coconut trees swayed and tossed as if in a trance. In my ears the roaring waves carried an echo of the Trichur festival music.

Several weeks later, I rode the ferry from Alleppey to Kottayam through the teeming backwaters, their level higher than that of the paddy fields – in a tropical version of the dikes of Holland. I drove through the mist and rain of the High Range, in the Western Ghats, where workers picked leaves in terraced tea gardens; on the way down, the road ran through plantations of pepper, cardamom and cinnamon. It was a journey through a spice-scented garden. The dense green of the foliage was relieved by monsoon-fed cascades and streams, which would join some of Kerala's forty-one rivers flowing towards the Arabian Sea. The rainy season lasts for three months.

While the Trichur Pooram heralds the south-west monsoon, the Onam festival, in September, signals its end. Onam is the most important Malayali celebration, honouring Mahabali, the mythical king who visits Kerala once a year. Coinciding with the harvest, it is a ten-day tableau of song, dance and family reunions providing a grand finale to the rains. Like Christians heading home for Christmas, Malayalis flock home for Onam. Planes and trains are packed during these holidays.

On the first day, a clay figure called *Onathappan*, a representation of Mahabali, is set up in household yards. It is decorated with ten tiers of flowers, one for each day of the festival, and children replace the faded flowers every morning. In the home the celebrations reach a climax on the last day, when new shirts, sarongs and saris are worn, gifts are given and a sumptuous meal prepared. On this day, in the home of my friend Jaya Prakash Paliath, in a village on the Menacil river, I ate an early meal specially cooked for me and served on fresh banana leaves. This delicious lunch consisted of *pulissery* (a chutney of coconut and curd), fish *mooli* (a stew with vegetables and onions in a coconut sauce), *kootu* (a mélange of mixed vegetables), a morsel of mango chutney, steaming rice, and *payyasom*, a dessert of rice and jaggery. The food was downed with water delicately flavoured with *geera-kam*, a herb with cleansing qualities.

I ate well but lightly because I had a four-hour drive ahead to Aranmulla, on the Pampa river, to watch the snake-boat regatta. Nothing like this water festival exists in the Asia through which I had travelled, and for someone like me, brought up in a desert state, Kerala's waterways had an enchanting quality.

When I reached the Vishnu Temple at Aranmulla, the boat with a prow like a bird's head – honouring Garuda, the vehicle of Vishnu – was out on the river. It made the Pampa look like something out of a mythical past. On the far bank was a row of parading elephants, a manifestation of the last white monsoon clouds that were still scattered in the sky. Crowds lined the banks watching the *Chundan Vallams*, the 130-foot-long, low-prowed snake-boats, whose 20-foot-high sterns tower over smaller boats. Police launches were prodding packed private boats onto the sides. A pageant of dancers, musicians and folk artists appeared in procession on boats and barges. Then the competition for smaller boats began. Some of them capsized, lending excitement to the event. Finally, the snake-boats were lined up, each with 120 men, almost all oarsmen. They raced with paddles moving in unison and singing to the rousing rhythm of their respective *Vanchipattu* or boat-songs. The crowd were shouting and clapping. At the end, the last light of the day was reflected from the silver-plated cups and shields of the winners.

The Onam festival also provided me with an opportunity to witness a variety of performances in Trivandrum. I was lucky to have as a companion the enthusiastic and knowledgeable Kavalam Narayan Pannicker, the leading playwright and director in Kerala, who helped me to understand not only all the many dances of the region, but, above all,

Kalaripayattu, the martial art of South India. This art is as old as, if not older than, its sister arts in the Far East. In fact, it is believed in the Far East that some martial arts and meditation were introduced to the area, through China, in the early sixth century, by a South Indian Buddhist monk.

Performers, arts and crafts

I later tracked down some of the artists in their own rural surroundings. Near Alleppey, I witnessed the nocturnal Sarpam Thullal, a devotional dance in which a fine *kalam* (floor-drawing) of one of Kerala's more popular and older deities, the *naga*, or snake, was drawn with rice powder, turmeric, lime and burned husk of paddy. A woman who was past the usual betrothal age invoked the snake-god to bless her with an early marriage. A Pullavan, who is not only a *kalam*-artist, but also a priest and singer, assisted by his wife, sang and played a primitive string instrument in praise of the *naga*. The woman twisted and turned on the floor in a trance and was joined in this act by her brother and uncle. At the end of the performance they rubbed out the drawing with their writhing bodies, and the water of a hundred coconuts was poured on them to cool them down.

South of Trivandrum, and on the track of other arts, I visited the elegant eighteenth-century Padmanabhapuram Palace where the Travancore rajas once lived. It is India's finest wooden building and has a striking affinity with the architecture of Kyoto. I was also taken by the dramatic and simple lines of the Vaikam Temple and the temples of Trichur district. I saw the stylized murals in the Dutch-built Mattancherry Palace, as well as in the Ettumanur Temple and at the Vishnu Temple in Midayikkunnu. At the Vazhapalli Siva Temple the Ramayana story is told in seventeenth-century wood sculpture. A rival version in the Vishnu Temple at Tiruvalla has inventive woodwork.

Among craftsmen, I visited the Palghat village home of

Kandan Moosari, the national award-winning bell-metal worker. I watched him and his son fashion a *charraku*, a large vessel for cooking rice dessert in temples. They also make household vessels. Elsewhere in Kerala I saw some of the area's old ivory carving and noted that along with murals, wood sculpture and traditional architecture, its time is past. Even some of the techniques have been lost, like that of making the black polished-plaster floor of the Padmanabhapuram Palace. All we know is that the white of eggs and burned coconut shells were used.

Kerala's traditional art mirrors its geography perfectly. Without exception the art is small-scale. It is usually viewed at eye-level and always projects a sense of intimacy. It is as if it were created within the closed confines of a coconut or cardamom grove. Only in the performing arts does it attain epic proportions, but without losing any of its sense of intimacy. Blessed with visual and musical magnificence, the performing arts of Kerala afford both spectacular sights and spectacular sounds. Collectively and in their own way – in a state which has no monumental architecture – they measure up to the artistic heights of Ellora, Ajanta and Konarak. Nowhere else in India do the performing arts equal the grandeur of Kathakali, Koodiyattam or the Teyyam dance.

'A Madhouse of Caste'

Just as the art and geography of Kerala differ vastly from those of any other part of India, so do its people and their caste system. Outside of Kerala, the Brahmins and the Kshatriyas, the warriors, have traditionally been at the peak of the pyramid, enjoying power and prestige. In the middle were the Vaishyas, who were traders, merchants, craftsmen and farmers. At the base were the Sudras, or menial workers, and tribesmen. And on the underside of the base, outside the caste structure, were the untouchables, who could pollute any of the upper castes by touch.

In Kerala, only the Namboodiris were at the peak. Below them were non-Malayali Brahmins, Kshatriyas (but not Kerala's warrior caste) and Ambalavasis or temple servants. There was no middle level in the pyramid – that is, no Vaishyas – the mercantile, trading and shopkeeping jobs being performed by Syrian Christians, Muslims, Jews and some non-Malayalis. The Nairs or warriors were Sudras and near the base. At the base itself were the polluting castes, the largest of whom were the Ezhavas, who were tappers and tenders of coconut palm. On the underside were the slave castes.

Pollution had been refined to an extraordinary degree in Kerala, through a combination of sight and distance. For instance, Namboodiris considered themselves atmospherically polluted if they saw a slave a hundred yards away. To cleanse themselves they performed purificatory rites. A Nair could not normally touch a Namboodiri. An Ezhava had to remain about forty paces from a Nair and a slave at least sixty-six paces.

The Namboodiris lived, cut off from the world, in high-walled houses called *illams* – sprawling mansions of wood, thatch and tile. Their estates were managed by Nairs or non-Malayali Brahmins, who in turn lorded it over tenants and slaves. The Namboodiri system allowed the eldest son to marry, but other sons and daughters were discouraged from marrying and the daughters were expected to remain virgins. But this system, though it kept family property together, necessarily resulted in a small Namboodiri population.

The Nairs followed the *marumakkattayam* or matrilineal system, whereby property was common and could not be divided. It was inherited through the female line. All members of a *tarawad* (the family home made of wood and tile) were the descendants of a single female ancestor. But the eldest male in the *tarawad*, called the *karanavar*, managed the family affairs. Married or unmarried Nair women had the sexual freedom to form several liaisons, first with

Namboodiris, then with other Nairs of the same status and with Kshatriyas. Nair marriages were entered into and ended with ease. Husbands did not belong to their wives' *tarawads*. They came after dinner and returned to their mothers' *tarawads* before breakfast.

From 1900 to Indian independence, the caste pyramid began to topple. The society which had lived unchanged for centuries and which was described early in this century as a 'madhouse of caste' turned into the most egalitarian society in India. This remarkable change was brought about by the introduction of ideas of equality, rising literacy, competition from other religions, missionary activity, the quest for social elevation by the deprived classes, land reforms, the breaking of commercial monopolies and the forward-looking political parties – a combination of factors that was special to Kerala.

The Ezhavas, who were once at the base of the pyramid, now rose to the top for several additional reasons: their numerical strength, the demand for coconut products which helped many of them to build fortunes and the arrival of reformists like the great Ezhava leader Sree Narayan Guru. On the other hand, the Namboodiris, because of their sheer lack of numbers and their orthodoxy, lost their former position of power. Yet it was Elamkulam Mana Sankaran, a Namboodiri, who led the Communists to victory in the first elections and introduced significant social reforms, a year after Kerala was formed in 1956.

Among the Namboodiris, I visited an *illam* in Palghat where some of the positive and intellectual pursuits of Namboodiri life are still practised. O.M.C. Narayana Namboodiripad, the 75-year-old noted Rig-Veda scholar and his family own Olappamana, an *illam* set in the shade of tropical trees. He lives there with his wife and some of his sons. He told me: 'It is stipulated in the Rig-Veda that you should have ten children, so I have ten children.' According to him, this epic of Aryan lore in 10,722 verses, which he learned by heart before the age of 14, was compiled 5,000 years ago, though he says European scholars date it back only to 2,000 years. O.M.C. has translated the entire Rig-Veda from Sanskrit to Malayalam, working seven hours a day for seven years. At his own expense, he has published four volumes of the translation, with over a thousand pages in each. Another four volumes are still to be published and the cost of these will be underwritten by the government. 'But,' commented O.M.C, 'the government is slow.'

I had arrived at Olappamana in time for the birthday ceremony of O.M.C.'s grandson, whose father works in Muscat, in the Middle East. In the rambling and grand house, beneath worm-eaten portraits of ancestors, a powerful image of Bhadrakali had been drawn in a style very similar to the snake *kalam* I had seen near Alleppey. This ceremony was called *Kalam Pattu*. The drawing had been made by 82-year-old Rama Kurup and his grandson, who belong to a caste of performers and *kalam* artists. A drummer beat on the *chenda*. The older Kurup played a three-string plucked instrument and sang in praise of the Mother Goddess.

Namboodiris and Ayurveda

The Namboodiris are known as patrons and practitioners of learning, of the arts and of Ayurveda – the traditional Indian science of life, vitality, health and longevity. Ayurveda places emphasis on the body and the person; the body's relationship to the natural environment and to the cosmos; its relationship to time; its psychic role, its unconscious levels and its material and social *milieu*. These considerations lead to the skilful use of pharmacological products, proper behaviour, dietetics, massage and medication. Ayurveda's concept of healing – evolved from an Oriental understanding of the laws of nature and life – is different from Occidental medicine. Unlike Western medicine – introduced to India in the eighteenth century – Ayurveda has maintained an unbroken contact with its ancient roots. A verse in the *Caraka Samhita*, one of the ancient treatises on Ayurveda, says: 'Mind, soul and body – these three are like a tripod; the world is sustained by their combination: they constitute the substratum for everything.'

In the commercial area of any Kerala town, there are shops selling roots, tubers and herbs. They look incongruous beside those selling plastic buckets, radios, television sets, bicycles and videos. Nevertheless, the Ayurveda products are a part of everyday life. The Ayurveda physician is readily available anywhere in Kerala, as elsewhere in India. The Arya Vaidya Sala (hospital) at Kottakal, near Calicut, is known nationally. Here patients from all over the country come for cures, including purification programmes in which effusions of oil and sweat-producing massages with balls of rice are used, notably for stress-related disorders and general physical and mental exhaustion. Ramnath Goenka, the old but energetic publisher of India's largest circulating English-language daily newspaper, told me: 'A few weeks at Kottakal added five years to my life. I wish I had the time to go for another cure.'

Nowadays Ayurveda practitioners have begun to adapt Western concepts, just as the West has begun to take note of Ayurveda. In Kottayam Dr N. S. Vayaskara Mooss, a 74-year-old Namboodiri, has combined his knowledge of medicinal plants, ancient Ayurvedic literature and a deep interest in modern botany. I visited him in a house set in an untended garden of plants and creepers. He is lean and wiry. His front teeth are missing and his tongue is coated red from chewing betel-leaf and betel-nut. He sat at a desk with a green plastic tablecloth, surrounded by cabinets full of books and shelves with stacks of papers. On a wall hung a calendar of photographs, showing a different orchid for every month. He peered at me from behind thick lenses. As I looked at one of his books, he informed me that he had printed it himself on a 1937 Monopoly treadmill letterpress. Sitting there, I glanced at the *Ganas of Vahata*, an English translation of an ancient Ayurvedic treatise. What struck me were the technical notes, the botanical identifications with local and Latin names, suggesting a lifetime's love of collecting, sampling and identifying plants.

Dr Mooss told me that eight families of Namboodiris traditionally practised Ayurveda since the god Parasurama reclaimed Kerala from the sea. He believes his family is descended from one of those original physicians. Apparently only three of these families are extant, though there are disciples who have passed on the tradition through the ages. Dr Mooss's views are conservative and pessimistic. He predicts that one day there will be no practitioners of Ayurveda left.

According to legend, the Namboodiris were the original inhabitants of Kerala. Parasurama, the axe-bearing incarnation of Vishnu, carved Kerala out of the sea by the throw of his axe. Land arose along the path of the axe. Parasurama first brought some Brahmins to live in Kerala, but they were frightened of snakes and did not stay long. He then brought the Namboodiris, gave them customs and manners, and settled them in sixty-four villages, where common people also came to live. A king was chosen and the first Chera kingdom established. It was during the rule of the later Cheras, when their capital shifted to Cranganore, that Christianity came to India. Some of the Namboodiris were the first converts.

Christianity

'The rulers of Malabar conferred 72 privileges on the early Syrian Christians. They had a social status traditionally equal to the Brahmins and were held in such high regard that if an untouchable defiled something, a Syrian Christian was asked to purify it by touch,' the Revd Dr K. V. Mathew of the Mar Thoma Church in Kottayam told me, adding, 'Christianity in Kerala is believed to be at least as old as, if not older than, Rome, according to the St Thomas tradition.'

Legend has it that St Thomas founded seven congregations in Kerala before he was supposedly speared to death by a Brahmin at Madras. There a shrine honours him. With the arrival of the trader Cana Thomas, leading a group of four hundred families from East Syria, in 345, history picks up the story of Christianity in India. Cana Thomas's followers intermingled with the St Thomas Christians. From this early beginning up to the fifteenth century, Syro-Chaldean priests presided over the rites of the Kerala Christians.

There was then a dramatic development. Vasco da Gama landed near Calicut in Malabar in 1498 in search of 'Christians and spices'. For the St Thomas Christians a new chapter opened. The Portuguese, who practised the Latin rite, saw the Oriental rites as heretical and an era of persecution began. In 1599 the Portuguese forced the majority of the St Thomas Christians to embrace an adaptation of the Latin rite, known as the Romo-Syrian rite, through an agreement called the Synod of Diamper. The small minority who escaped this rite continue today as the 30,000-member Chaldean Church, with Indian headquarters in Trichur and paying allegiance to the Patriarch at Baghdad.

But the Portuguese provocations continued, and led in 1653 to a confrontation. About 25,600 Christians faced the cruel colonizers at Cochin Fort, before retreating to Mattancherry. There they took the oath: 'We and our children shall never bow to Rome.' They had already sought to revive their tenuous ties with the Orthodox churches in Antioch, Babylon, Jerusalem, Alexandria and Abyssinia. In the meantime, other rival European powers had reached Kerala. The Dutch defeated the Portuguese in 1663 and eased the pressure on the Syrian Christians. Over a century later, the Dutch were in turn defeated by the English, who published a Malayalam translation of the Gospel in 1811 and five years later opened the first Anglican seminary in Kerala.

Only recently have Western clergymen begun to recognize Christianity's Eastern foundation. The Revd Dr Mathew reminded me: 'Christianity began as an Oriental religion. This cassock I am wearing is an Arab dress which I bought in Dubai. Our caps, beards and many of our manners are west Asian.'

Today, the Nestorians, the Chaldeans, some Cannanites and one faction of the Syrian Orthodox Church have links with west Asia. The head of the Jacobite Syrian Orthodox Church is the Patriarch of Antioch, who lives in Damascus. The other major faction, the Malankara* Orthodox Syrian Church, is Indianized. The Mar Thoma Church has the Metropolitan of Tiruvalla as its head but maintains liturgical links with the Anglican Church. The Catholic Church, besides its Latin rite, has the Syro-Malabar or Romo-Syrian rite, going back to the Synod of Diamper, and the Malankara Syrian rite, dating to the early twentieth century, when a faction of the Orthodox Syrian Church turned to Catholicism.

There are, of course, other churches in Kerala: the Pentecostals, the Lutherans, the Brethren Mission and the Church of God, some of which have several factions.

For members of the Catholic Church in Kerala, the most momentous occasion of recent years was the visit of Pope John Paul II to Kerala, during his ten-day tour of India in February. The Pope was propagating a 'Call to Unity'. Big crowds were expected in Kerala, a state that boasts more than half of the entire 11 million Christian population of India. Kerala's Catholics alone number 3 million. The Pope was visiting Kottayam to perform the beatification of a Kerala priest and nun, the first such ceremony in India. I had imagined that the crowd would match one of the gatherings on the Ganges.

At dawn the orderly Malayalis, wearing clean white shirts, sarongs and saris, began filing into the stadium where the beatification was to be held. Many of the men sported papershades advertising 'Shalimar Jewellery'. They passed beneath

---

* Malankara is the island, off Cranganore, where St Thomas is believed to have landed.

giant portraits of the Pope, banners bearing his name, bunting fluttering in the wind and commercial signs such as 'Breezy Welcome To His Holiness The Pope – Polar, The Super Fan.' I scanned the amphitheatre – neatly circled by coconut palms but marred by gaudy buildings at the edges – just before the Pope was about to arrive. The crowds were poor, only half filling the stadium. Then there were shouts of 'Jai Popurajan, Victory for the Pope King!' and a choir burst into a song welcoming the head of the Catholic Church to the soil of Kottayam.

The Pope set an historic precedent for the Catholic churches of Kerala by excluding the Latin rite and performing the Holy Mass for the first time in the Syro-Malabar rite, to which the two Venerables, Revd Fr Kuriakose Elias Chavara and Sister Alphonsa Muttathupadathu, belonged. Halfway through the Mass, the Pope pronounced the nineteenth-century priest and nun '. . . raised to the ranks of the blessed in the great communion of saints'. The long process of beatification had begun thirty years before. The Vatican would continue to watch for acceptable miracles caused by the intercession of the two Blesseds before declaring them saints.

The Pope then drove from the stadium to meet members of the Malankara Orthodox Syrian sect at the Mar Elia Cathedral. There, the head of the hierarchy, the Catholicos, Mar Baselios Marthoma Mathews I, embraced the Pope and, after some small formalities, raised the old controversy between the Oriental and the Catholic Church. After speaking of the privilege he felt as the 'successor' of the Apostle St Thomas to welcome, for the first time in history, the 'successor' of the Apostle St Peter, he reminded his listeners that until five centuries ago there was but one church in India, but '. . . today the children of St Thomas are sadly divided.' These divisions, the Catholicos maintained, were brought from the West, and he urged the Pope to put an end to the 'sheep-stealing and proselytizing'. 'Who will heal centuries of old wounds?' he asked. A part of the Pope's reply was widely quoted: 'You are the Pope of Kottayam and I am the Pope of Rome.'

The Syrian Christians, who make up about three-quarters of the Christian population of Kerala, have a special identity. Their customs and manners are different from those of other Christians. There is a marked difference between many of their names and those used in the west, thus, Thomas is Mammen, Peter is Oommen, Paul is Peeli, Elizabeth is Eliamma, Mary is Mariamma or Mariakutty and Sara is Saramma or Sarakutty.

When a Syrian Christian is born, horoscopes are still drawn up by the astrologer. Arranged marriages are not uncommon, and in the marriage ceremony the ring is less important than the *tali*, a small gold cross strung on a piece of string. The bridegroom knots this around the bride's neck and she wears it as a symbol of her betrothal.

Junior priests are allowed to marry and can eat meat. But only those who remain unmarried can rise to the ranks of the Metropolitans and the Catholicos, and all hierarchs have to be vegetarians. The stamp of the East is evident on many of the Syrian Christian practices. Western proselytizing priests, from the Portuguese to the English, have in the past been shocked at the multiracial character and Indianized customs of the Syrian Christians. The Revd Samuel Mateer of the London Missionary Society wrote in his 1883 book, *Native Life in Travancore*: 'The ignorance and spiritual darkness of these nominal Christians is very great . . .'

What would the Revd Mateer make of 34-year-old Annama Verghese and her family? I met her in the house in which she works as a part-time maid on the outskirts of Kottayam. She, her sister and two brothers were baptized and brought up as Catholics. She married a Hindu, who then converted to Catholicism. After his sudden death Annama joined the Indian Pentecostal Church. Her eldest son has a Hindu name, Jai Mon, and is raised as a Hindu by her in-laws. She brings up her other son herself as a Pentecostal. Her sister and two brothers married Hindus and converted to Hinduism. They pray at Guruvayur and other temples. Annama's parents remain loyal to the Catholic faith. I asked Annama whether the diverse beliefs of its members caused any friction in the family. 'No,' she responded easily, 'everyone does what he or she wants to do. We don't interfere with each other.'

'Liberation Theology' and the Fisherman's Agitation

Private paradoxes are common in Kerala, yet they allow harmony. But public paradoxes and perennial problems bedevil the state. Annama's former place of worship, the Catholic Church, for example, has a problem the likes of which Annama could never have imagined.

In 1954, trawlers were introduced to Kerala, under an Indo-Norwegian project, even though at that time trawling was prohibited in Norway and other Western countries. There are 2,500 trawlers in Kerala today. They work, almost exclusively, the in-shore and off-shore zone and not the deep sea for which they are meant. Only 5 per cent of the state's fishing is done in the deep sea. Using heavy beams, the trawlers scrape the sea bed and haul up vast quantities of young, useless fish. They destroy spawn, especially in the breeding season – the south-west monsoon – and they disturb the sea-floor ecology. As a result, many varieties of fish and prawn have completely disappeared. The total catch dropped dramatically from 400,000 tonnes in 1974 to 270,000 tonnes in 1981.

Kerala's 80,000 active and traditional fishermen have been hit hard by the state's ecological mismanagement. With the disappearing forests, the price of their country-craft had already shot up to Rs.20,000.00 ($1660.00) for big ones, forcing the fishermen to pool their resources to purchase the boats collectively. The rising prices drove many fishermen into other jobs or into unemployment. When the trawlers arrived, the fishermen, disturbed by this new danger to the very potential of fishing, organized strikes, road-blocks, marathon fasts, and demonstrations. Occasionally, trawlers out at sea were set on fire. Christian nuns and priests often led the protesting fishermen, who also had the support of the Communist parties.

Aided by these two groups, the fishermen organized themselves into unions and co-operatives, and put forward three demands: a ban on trawling during the south-west monsoon months; a ban on trawling in the in-shore zone; and a ban on night trawling. The government conceded the last two demands, simply because the Marine Regulation Act already prohibited them and the fishermen were in fact only asking for the law to be enforced. As for the first demand, the government agreed to reduce the number of trawlers to 1,150, arguing that shrimps were most plentiful during the monsoon months. On the part of the government, however, the whole exercise was academic. The trawlers continue to ply today in full force. They are owned by the government and by vested interests.

In the meantime, 'liberation theology' entered the picture. Conceived in the slums of Latin America by Christian priests, this philosophy held that the traditional profession of preaching should be put aside when the needs of the poor called for activist participation. In some Malayali seminaries, this radical theology had already gained acceptance. But its public prominence came only with the fishermen's agitation.

The Marxists, through newspaper and magazine articles, warmly applauded the arrival of liberation theology on the soil of Kerala; the hierarchs of the Catholic Church, on the other hand, grew alarmed. They saw it not as a support for the oppressed fisherman but rather as another spawning ground for the Marxist-led Opposition Front. However, the moral stance of the Catholic Church was perhaps not altogether pure, because the Church is universally believed to be a powerful partner in propping up the shaky coalition government, the United Front, through its supposedly political arm, the Kerala Congress – a party of rich Christian plantation owners and businessmen. The crusading nuns and priests were either transferred or ordered out of the agitations – exactly as had been the case in South America.

Islam

Islam, like Christianity, came to Kerala through Cranganore and the spice trade. Arab sailors and traders married local women, some conversions took place, and the Mappila or Malabar Muslim population was forged. It is one of the oldest Islamic communities in South Asia.

Through the Red Sea and the Mediterranean, the Arabs and the Malabar merchants supplied spices to Arabia, Egypt, and Turkey, as well as to Venice, which with Genoa had taken over Roman trade. The Venetians in turn sold spices to other Europeans. Then a rival trading power and a rival route created a crisis.

In 1498, the Portuguese outflanked the ancient route and reached Malabar by rounding the Cape of Good Hope, with the intention of capturing the coveted trade and setting up a spicery in Lisbon. There was panic in both Venice and Malabar. 'To the city of St Mark, the loss of the spice trade "would be like the loss of milk to a new-born babe",' writes the noted French historian Fernand Braudel,* quoting a contemporary Venetian observer. In Malabar, the Portuguese threat to monopolize the maritime trade and also religiously to suppress the Mappila merchants and seamen provoked a bitter hundred-year armed struggle. Patrols, blockades, clashes and confrontations ensued. The Portuguese left a legacy of hatred that would have a lasting and militant effect on the Mappilas. Throughout the colonial period, the Mappilas remained restless underdogs. In this century, their unrest climaxed in the Mappila Rebellion of 1921-22 which challenged colonial rule

* Fernand Braudel, *The Mediterranean World in the Age of Philip II, Vol. I (Economies: Trade and Transport)*, London and Paris, 1966.

and Hindu landlordism. It led eventually to the political organization of the Kerala Muslims, that is, to the forming of the Muslim League and the carving out of the Muslim-majority district of Malappuram – the latter agreed to by E.M.S. and his Communist government in 1969. Today, the Kerala Muslims make up 20 per cent of the state's population. They are mainly traders and agriculturists.

I was familiar with the Muslim culture of North India, and I noted in my travels through Malabar that Mappila culture was quite different, as their history has been different. The trading Mappilas do not have the political, bureaucratic, military or aristocratic legacy that North Indian Muslims have inherited from the Afghans and Moghuls. Nor do they have the musical and the visual art tradition that evolved out of North Indian court life. But they do have their *Mappila Pattu* – Arabi-Malayalam poems and songs largely dealing with religious topics and the history of Islam. There is also a poem which compares conditions under the Zamorins, the tolerant rulers of Calicut, with those that prevailed under the intolerant Portuguese.

What I found particularly fascinating in Mappila culture were their traditional wooden mosques. Not many are left now, as the trend is either to build new ones or to rebuild old ones in the Mecca style. Still, the mosques in Calicut, Kasargode, Tirurangadi and a few other places have survived. In these, wood is lavishly used and there are no minarets. The pulpits are exquisitely carved. The facades have decorated gables like those of Kerala's Hindu temples, and in fact both the wooden mosques and the temples were built by Hindu carpenters and masons. The Kuttichira Mosque in Calicut looks rather like a large wooden ship with a deep hold for cargo, and the nearby palm trees swaying in the breeze suggest wind-whipped sails. I was reminded of the long history of Mappila trade.

The Kuttichira Mosque is close to the Calicut seafront, an area of tile and wood warehouses; courtyards, where pepper and other plantation products are sifted and sorted out; and porches, with white pillars, where merchants laze. On the sea, facing the weathered waterfront, country-craft with billowing sails are reminiscent of centuries of Malabar pirates. Pliny the Elder complained of them. But in Portuguese times, these pirates proudly fought the cruel colonizers. In the late seventeenth century, the notorious Captain Kidd began his career of crime in the Calicut waters by seizing a Dutch bark and then a Muslim vessel of 400 tons with a prized cargo. His piracy plagued the Malabar Coast until he sailed off for the New World. (He was eventually hanged at Tilbury gaol).

But behind the waterfront, in the crowded bazaars, there is little to suggest Calicut's colourful past, though there are enough stores selling cloth to remind us that this is the city from whose cotton textiles the word calico was coined. Sweetmeat street is in the heart of this congested area. There, Kousar Stores stands alongside stationers, clothiers, electrical goods shops and news vendors. This shop has pink plastic show-cases and show-windows displaying frocks, négligés, sweaters and other women's and children's clothes. The proprietor sits at a desk, below an ornate wall clock and a calendar advertising baby's formula. Beside him is a bright red telephone. He is C.N. Ahmed Maulvi, a slight and be-spectacled man of 81. He is a trader, a farmer and an intellectual, famous in Kerala for his liberal views and his scholarly books, especially his five-volume translation of the Koran.

Ahmed Maulvi believes that in modern Mappila society there is far less orthodoxy than there is in the north. 'For example,' he says, 'our women do not use the burqa or the veil. They work in the fields. We can now boast of Muslim engineers and doctors. The Muslim Education Society and the Muslim Service Society run hospitals, orphanages, commercial training colleges and arts and science colleges. We even have a Muslim woman as a High Court judge.' With regard to communalism and politics, he is, he said, proud to have fought the mullahs through his books. 'The Muslim League uses the orthodoxy to obtain votes. However, in daily life there is little communalism in Kerala, because Islam came here peacefully through trade; unlike the north, where it was established mostly through conquest. There is much cooperation among Kerala's different communities. Only the politicians are communal-minded.'

Politics: Communalism and Communism

Kerala's politics has the force of an assaulting monsoon wave. I first began taking note of the state's communal-politics soon after my arrival in 1982, when I began this book. One day, I took a taxi from Trivandrum to Cochin. Captivated by the beauty of the coastline, I was in a day-dream, but was suddenly jolted out of it by a line of cars coming around a bend at breakneck speed. After my driver had barely managed to avoid a collision, I asked him, 'Who are these madmen?' He laughed and replied, as if this were an everyday occurrence: 'Government toppling, sir! Chief Minister rushing for meeting.' The next morning the newspapers revealed that the government had indeed been saved by some bizarre horse-trading in the dead of night.

Democracy in Kerala is not a neat two-lane highway. It is a narrow and bumpy road, on which few rules are followed. In the early 1980s, I began to watch with some interest the fortunes of the United Democratic Front coalition government, formed after the 1982 elections. In the eyes of the press and the public its composition is communal. The partners led by India's ruling party, the Congress (I), are: the Kerala Congress, believed to be backed by the Catholic Church; the Indian Union Muslim League; the National Democratic Party, formed by the Nair community; the Socialist Republican Party, formed by a small faction of the Ezhava community; and two unique one-man parties, with both 'leaders' enjoying ministerships. It is commonly believed that the United Democratic Front carved out the district of Pathanamthitta in 1984 to satisfy one single elected politician, who was not even a minister.

The opposition, the Left Democratic Front, led by the Communist Party of India (Marxist) has an almost equally communal composition. Its other members are the Communist Party of India; the Janata Party; and the Revolutionary Socialist Party. The All India Muslim League quit this coalition after the Marxists assailed the *Shariat* (the Muslim personal law) in 1985.

No single party was able to win a majority in the seven elections to the state assembly, except in 1957, when the Communists won overwhelmingly. Thirteen governments have been formed in thirty years. President's Rule – a non-elected caretaker administration under a Governor appointed by New Delhi – has been imposed seven times. In one remarkable four-year period – 1977 to 1980 – six ministries and five Chief Ministers were sworn in. From the first elections until today, just one government has completed its full five-year term of office.

The Communists have been the most striking political force in Kerala since the formation of the state. The factors which give Communism its appeal to Keralites, especially in Malabar, are a combination of literacy, highly unionized labour, agrarian relations, land ownership and material and social benefits.

The Communist Party was founded in 1931 by former followers of Mahatma Gandhi and the Congress Socialists. It did not have the terrorist origins of the West Bengal Communists. When E.M.S., one of the early members of the party, and others embarked on a brief terrorist adventure in the late forties, it was short-lived and so unsuccessful that the party has since steered clear of Maoist-style activism, in favour of Kerala's highly complex ballot-box politics.

Twenty-eight months after their 1957 election success, Kerala's Communists were pushed out of government by the 'liberation struggle' organized by the Congress Party, the Catholic Church and others. Communist inroads on land-owning vested interests and Communist educational reforms look bland today because successive governments have followed E.M.S.'s lead and have given hundreds of thousands of peasants their own small plots to cultivate. But when the reforms were introduced, they roused powerful opposition. President's Rule was declared. Then, in 1964, the Communist Party split into two camps: the 'pro-Peking' Communist Party of India (Marxist), abbreviated to CPI(M), and the 'pro-Soviet' Communist Party of India, known as CPI. In the same year, the Communists' main opponents, the Congress Party, also split. These divisions, as well as other political fragmentations, paved the way for Kerala's successive coalition governments. Nevertheless, at least one faction of the Communists remained in government almost continuously between 1967 and 1981.

Mr and Mrs T.V. Thomas best exemplified the ideological split in the Communist ranks.* Mrs Thomas, a formidable and unsentimental woman, and a member of CPI(M), coolly dismissed her husband, a CPI follower, as a 'revisionist' and a 'bourgeois opportunist', while a pained Mr Thomas deplored his wife's 'dogmatism'. When the Communist-dominated coalition took office in 1967, Mrs Thomas was appointed Food Minister and Mr Thomas Industries Minister. During the allocation of ministerial housing, it was noticed with surprise that the Thomases took separate, though adjacent, houses. During the day, the Thomases shared their separate ideologies with their friends and fellow travellers at their respective residences. At night, Mrs Thomas locked up her house and went next door. Her husband explained: 'She makes sure I eat only the right foods. She is a very good wife.'

During my time in Kerala, it did not surprise me that I never heard of 'the struggle to liberate the masses' or of the

* Joseph Lelyveld, 'Communism Kerala Style', *New York Times Magazine*, April 1967.

'threat of neocolonialism'. But I was surprised at how often I was told of Communism's fascinating interaction with Hinduism. Like the Communists who performed the Guruvayur *thulabharam*, many Marxists make the pilgrimage to Sabarimalai, the mountain temple honouring Kerala's most popular god, Ayyappa, the offspring of Siva and Vishnu. In a similar vein, there is the example of the Vannan of Malabar. This 'low-caste' community perform Teyyams – literally 'God's dance' – yet are staunch Communists.

Teyyam: 'God's Dance'

In most Teyyam performances, Bhadrakali, the Mother Goddess, is worshipped. Others honour folk heroes, mythological and legendary characters, spirits, other gods and sometimes even Muslim figures harking back to the days of the sailing ships and the spice trade. There are more than 400 varieties of Teyyam. Bright, colourful costumes which help to invoke the divine spirit are worn. The performer is not only practised in music, mysticism, martial art, make-up, acting and choreography, but is also deeply versed in mythology. He (there are no female Teyyam practitioners) dances to the mesmerizing music of the *chenda*, of cymbals and of pipes. Hymns and songs are sung, flowers offered, oil lamps and flame-torches lit and swords and shields flourished.

Teyyams are performed for the prosperity of persons and villages and to ask blessings on property. They are also used to fulfil vows or to offer thanks in the event of prized Gulf-jobs. There can be a single performance with one or many participants or a whole festival lasting for weeks; though most Teyyams are day-long affairs. Teyyams are a characteristic and essential component of the rural life of Malabar. The various districts are dotted with shrines for Teyyam worship.

The Teyyam is thought to be Dravidian in origin, with an incorporation of Aryan gods, a result of cultural contact between the two from 2 BC to the ninth century.* The Vannan, who perform most Teyyams, are mentioned in the oldest writings of South India, the Sangam literature, written in Tamil (200 BC to AD 300).

I watched 40-year-old Kuruvat Chindon, a Vannan, perform a Teyyam in the village of Payyanur in north Malabar. Like other Vannans, Chindon has hereditary ties to higher caste families in his village. The Teyyam I saw was ordered by a Nair who worked in the Middle East and had returned home temporarily to use his savings to build a small house. After the ceremony I talked to Chindon, a small, lithe man with sharp features and close-cropped hair. He told me he had performed the *Muthappan* (Siva) Teyyam. In this personification, Siva is an ordinary being, consuming toddy, fish and meat. Chindon remarked, 'These days, with rising prices, *Muthappan* is a very popular Teyyam, providing protection and aid in difficult times.'

Later, I visited Chindon's home, a slummy two-room house in a scanty coconut and cashew grove. The packed and pebbly soil, on which it stands, alone suggested the poverty of the place. The land was so barren that it did not even allow the growth of a kitchen garden. Extra space had been created by erecting walls of palm matting which were propped up against the overhanging roof. The smoke from the kitchen had turned these black. Inside the house the rooms were bare, except for some clothes slung on a line, and Teyyam accessories, such as drums, swords and shields. Chindon lived in these cramped quarters with his wife, three children, three sisters and two brothers-in-law.

The boom in Gulf houses allows Chindon to supplement his Teyyam income by undertaking construction work. He works about 120 days a year from 8 a.m. to noon, earning Rs.25.00 ($2.20) per day. For Teyyams he charges Rs.100.00 ($8.10) for a few hours of performance, though this sum is

---

* KK.N. Kurup, *The Cult of Teyyam and Hero Worship in Kerala*, Calcutta, 1972.

shared with the make-up artist and the drummer. Chindon's income varies from Rs.500.00 to Rs.1000.00 ($40.00 to $80.00) per month. His wife adds to their earnings by washing clothes for the Namboodiris, the Nairs and the Ezhavas, for which she makes Rs.500.00 ($40.00) per month. One of his sisters earns Rs.20.00 ($1.60) per day at a coir factory. Chindon's brothers-in-law are also Teyyam artists who undertake construction work. They also help with the household expenses.

The women in Chindon's family perform the traditional act of washing the menstruation clothes of Namboodiri and Nair women. They also provide the *mattu*, a purificatory cloth, on which the members of the upper castes will stand in ritual on the twelfth day after a birth or death in their family. For the Namboodiris and Nairs this ceremony is important, but for the Vannan the washing of clothes and the *mattu* ritual is debasing. It was with distress that Chindon talked of 'this slavery'.

But when Chindon spoke of his children, he was full of pride and delight. Two of his sons attend a primary school and his daughter, who is four, was to begin school the following year. He also told me that his wife could read and write Malayalam. He himself almost completed his secondary education and has learned a little English.

I turned the conversation finally to politics. Chindon insisted, 'My family complete CPI(M)! All CPI(M)!' But he could not explain why he votes for the Marxists, though it is an accepted fact that the depressed Vannans use Communism as an instrument of social elevation.

Y. V. Kannan is related to Chindon. A teacher and a part-time Teyyam artist, he lives, in contrast to his cousin, in a fertile area of Payyanur. His three-room house is spotless and stands on 1.25 acres of land with cashew and pepper trees. Literacy has given Kannan a different outlook from that of other Vannans. This short, stocky and intense high-school teacher now performs Teyyams only for pleasure. He holds a BA in Malayalam literature, as well as a Bachelor of Education diploma. Kannan tells me that among about 5,000 Vannans in the two northern districts of Malabar, there are roughly 50 college graduates. His own brother is a lecturer in physics. Kannan's salary is Rs.1,100.00 ($88.00) per month, while his brother draws Rs.1,500.00 ($120.00) per month.

Kannan talked with deep dignity: 'My father was a great Teyyam artist. I also love it, though purely as an art. I feel deeply for it. But there is no honour in it. While you perform, people touch your feet, they worship you, you are Everest; but after the performance you are nothing.' When the subject of politics was brought up, he told me that in the last elections he had voted for the CPI(M). When I suggested to him that his position vis-à-vis religion and Communism was perhaps paradoxical, he responded with sincerity: 'There is no contradiction between Teyyam and CPI(M).' In other words, the Mother Goddess and Marx are not mutually exclusive. That is Communism, Kerala style.

Literacy

As striking as Kerala's Communism is its passion for literacy. Kerala has been known for its intellectual pursuits since ancient times. The Sankaracharya's philosophy and preaching and Namboodiri scholarship established it as a leading centre of learning equal to Kashmir and Banaras. The mathematicians and astronomers of ancient and medieval Kerala were widely known. Aryabhata, who was evidently from Kerala, found out the value of π in 496, and Madhava, who lived in 1400, worked out its value to eleven decimal points. Today, 54-year-old E. C. George Sudarshan, who was born a Syrian Christian but is now a practising Hindu, is internationally known for his work in elementary particle physics.

Christianity had brought to Kerala its own zeal and enthusiasm for learning. Recently, there has been an exceptional rise in literacy in the traditionally backward Muslim area of Malappuram – registering the highest district-wise increase in the state since 1971. Social mobility and the competition among religious communities have both contributed to Kerala's high literacy rate: 76 per cent among men and 66 per cent among women. The national average is 35 per cent.

Kottayam is one of the centres of literary activity in India. Its literacy rate stands at 82 per cent. It is the home of India's largest circulating newspaper and magazine: the *Malayalam Manorama,* a daily that sells 634,000 copies, and the *Mangalam Weekly,* selling 1,300,00 copies. A total of 3,500,000 magazines are printed in Kottayam each week.

Kottayam is also the book publishing centre of Kerala, bringing out about 700 titles, including reprints, every year. The Sahitya Pravarthaka Co-operative Society (SPCS) alone issued 480 of them in 1985. Founded in 1945, the SPCS claims the distinction of being the world's first writers' co-operative. The present secretary, Gopi Kodungallur, told me, 'We pay a 30 per cent royalty to authors, while normal royalties in Kerala range from 5 per cent to 20 per cent.' The Society puts out a monthly bulletin for its 16,000 subscribers. It publishes dictionaries, encyclopaedias, basic reference works, poems and novels. The latter sell the least, with the exception of some of the works of the novelist Siva Sankara Pillai, Kerala's best known author and a founding member of the co-operative. *Chemmeem,* literally 'Shrimp', Pillai's fine novel about impoverished fishermen near Alleppey, published in 1956, is now in its nineteenth edition, with translations in fifty languages, in India and abroad.

One of the criticisms of the co-operative is that every Malayali now wants to be an author. In a recent year the reviewing committee had to read 2,000 manuscripts. The co-operative has 600 members who demand publication. In addition production costs have soared; royalties are high; and book sales have been hit by both the boom in television and the spectacular rise in magazine circulation.

The Economy

Kerala's literate electorate demands educational, medical and social benefits as well as decent wages. Forty-three per cent of the state's budget is spent on education. The rise in literacy has meant that of the 1 million unemployed, out of a work-force of 8 million, most are literate. But, paradoxically, wages have not fallen due to unemployment, even though the per capita income is below the national average. Yet there is no desperate poverty in Kerala. The working class is far better off there than their counterparts elsewhere in India, because income is more equitably divided. They are a frugal people with a simple lifestyle. On the street it is difficult to tell rich from poor. They combine a sense of modesty with great pride.

Sixteen per cent of the budget is spent on health services. Two doctors are posted in every *panchayat* (a rural administrative body or area manning a five- to ten-bed hospital). Kerala boasts India's lowest infant mortality rate: 40 deaths in rural and 34 in urban areas in every 1,000 births; while the national average stands at 124. Life expectancy exceeds the national average by 14 years. In family planning the state has registered an exemplary success. Malayali nurses are highly prized throughout India and now have even found a footing abroad.

This small state occupies only 1 per cent of the area of India, but supports almost 4 per cent of the country's population. It has an average density of 655 persons per sq.km. In parts of the coastal regions of southern Kerala the density shoots up to an extraordinary 1,500 persons per sq.km., making Kerala's countryside one of the most crowded in the world. The seaside road from Trivandrum to Cochin seems like one long street, while the Western Ghats, in contrast, are sparsely populated. Pressure of population has pushed 500,000 Malayalis to work outside the state, including 200,000 in the lucrative Middle East. The rush to the Gulf has left the state with a shortage of skilled workers, such as carpenters, electricians and plumbers. Though the Gulf boom is now declining, at its peak the remittances home had risen to a yearly 1,000 crore rupees ($830 million).

Little of this money was invested. Instead, much of it went into building houses, cinemas, and hotels or was simply put in the bank. Increased purchasing power pushed up prices, especially the price of land. One Gulf-returnee, when asked why he did not invest his savings, replied, 'Who can trust a government which can fall any day? Its successor could introduce different investment policies.' More important, Keralites returning from the Gulf are not of the entrepreneurial class and therefore do not take risks. Keralites in general have traditionally fought shy of the share market; investment in stock has a limited attraction for them. Business is conducted on a small-scale basis by families or by individuals. The Gulf-returnees have simply set themselves up for retirement and in the process brought inflation to the state.

The plantations are still the backbone of Kerala's economy, producing most of India's tapioca, lemon grass, cardamom, cinnamon, coconut, arecanut, pepper and rubber; and some of its coffee, cocoa and tea. Yet in its own food requirements Kerala is perennially short by 50 per cent. Most agricultural land is used for the cash crops. Less than 30 per cent is cultivated for paddy – an area in which there has been no growth in the last fifteen years. The state's yield per acre on food crops is one of the poorest in India. On a per capita basis, Kerala's foreign exchange earnings are the highest in the country due to its cash crop economy and Gulf-remittances.

Some industrialists consider Kerala's plantation owners to be advantaged in one respect: they employ the illiterate Tamil labour from across the border, who will work for low wages. In contrast, Kerala's literate labour, on the farm and in the factory, is considered uppity, undisciplined, highly unionized and agitational. The mere mention of Malayali labour gives heartburn to some industrialists. A non-Malayali employer bemoaned: 'God willing, I never see this place again.' Even a Malayali felt strongly enough to condemn his own state: 'Only sinners are born here. I hope I am never reborn in Kerala.'

The case of the Gwalior Rayon Silk Mills, a factory producing staple fibre and pulp, has become famous in Kerala. The first Communist government had encouraged the Birlas, a powerful Indian capitalist dynasty, to start this factory. Reportedly, raw material was offered to them at Rs.1.00 per ton. This deal later led to the election campaign cry that the Communists were in collusion with the capitalists. In the meantime Gwalior Rayon's workers boasted the state's highest industrial wages. Almost all of the factory's 4,000 workers were drawing a monthly salary of Rs.1,600.00 ($135.00) or more; while the average industrial wage in Kerala stood at Rs.1,000.00 ($85.00). In addition, a bonus exceeding 40 per cent was given to the workers. Then, three years ago, the bonus was suddenly and severely cut. The management's argument was that the factory was incurring a loss. The workers, in turn, contended that the proprietors had in fact made a six-fold profit on their initial investment. As a result, Gwalior Rayon was plagued by strikes. Negotiations were stalled because the management maintained that there was no point in discussing bonuses, wages and service conditions, when the future of the factory was in question.

Wood-based industries were in dire need of raw material and complained that the government had never supplied them with the promised tonnage. In the meantime, the government had set up its own rayon factory, to which it supplied wood at a fraction of the price paid by the private sector. Rival political parties became involved in the price fixing and wood supply. Soon the neighbouring states that had been selling wood to Gwalior Rayon and others banned its transport across their borders because India had implemented a new forest policy.

The mandarins in New Delhi had suddenly woken up to the fact that the forests had been destroyed. Kerala's own forest cover was down to a mere 15 per cent of the state's total land area. There had been proposals to allow the wood-based industries private plantations to cater to their needs, but these proposals were only partially implemented. What one government gave, its successor took back. In the end, Gwalior Rayon, which is under 'lay-off', was reduced to thinking of running the plant seasonally, like a sugar factory. Other industrialists simply packed their bags and left, to the benefit of the neighbouring states and to the detriment of Kerala's unemployed and under-employed labour.

Much of the blame for Kerala's sick industries is unfairly laid at the door of the unions. But a Gujarati industrialist, who had bought out two failing chemical concerns in Kerala and transformed them into successful companies, took a different view: 'We make a profit from extracting calcium from sea shells. Our success is due to management techniques which are different from those in other parts of India. We made an agreement linking high wages to production and contracted the work to the unions.' The truth is that medium-scale and small-scale industries run by imaginative managers have been singularly successful in Kerala. Nevertheless, Kerala's management-worker relations are so complex that one former electricity minister managed to hold membership of 33 labour unions.

Kerala: Another India

It is undeniable that Malayalis, with their high literacy, their skills and their legitimate demands for a better life, have placed themselves in a completely different league from any other Indian community. Therefore the state of Kerala needs a fresh and bold approach from both the industrialists and the government. Most of the paradoxes and problems of Kerala – like the fishermen's agitation – are the products, not primarily of the people, but of the politicians and vested interests.

There is much to admire about Kerala, in spite of its complex problems. This tiny state has much to teach the vast Indian subcontinent. In fact, Kerala is the only part of India where it is possible to talk of 'the quality of life'. Even a modest urban wage-earner can manage to own a house and a plot of land, for the countryside weaves in and out of each town. It is the only Indian state where there is an equitable relationship between rural and urban life. Its towns do not have the poverty or the industrial blight of the big Indian cities.

Kerala's colour is a god-given green, while that of the Indian Plain and the Deccan Plateau is a sun-baked brown. The Plain and the Plateau are dotted with ruins of caravanserais, forts, palaces, tombs and Moghul and Afghan monuments. Delhi alone has over a thousand of them. Their weathered stones and their cracked and crumbling plaster suggest the passage of a passionate and violent past. Even the northern and Deccan dust evokes for me images of marching armies, cannon smoke, the weariness of long journeys and the measured bullock-cart pace of time. Outside of Kerala, the whistle or the lights of a moving train suggest the immense Indian subcontinent. And the song of a Rajasthani folk singer I once heard on a railway platform accompanying himself with the lonesome music of the *sarangi* – has registered in my mind as a metaphor for the endless, arid stretches of my desert home-state. But Kerala is that strange and wonderful edge of India, with little dust, few ruins and modest but magnificent monuments. There, journeys are short, smooth and refreshingly clean. To this compact and neat ribbon of land nature applies a coat of green twice a year. Thus, in spite of its perennial problems, Kerala has a beguiling and beckoning look. Its freshness suggests that it has passed through centuries of civilization with the mere flutter of its green wings.

Captions

1. Country-craft ferrying plantation products; the sail is advertising tea; Cochin, the premier port of Kerala.
2. Ferry (foreground) plying between Fort Cochin and Willingdon Island where ships are docked.
3. Ferry on the Kottayam-Alleppey run, during the monsoon.
4. Lagoon on the outskirts of Alleppey.
5. View from a Kovalam beach hotel, near Trivandrum, the state capital.
6. Women collecting sand for construction in the bed of the sacred Bharatapuzha river.
7. Workers picking tea leaves in a High Range estate, bordering Kerala and Tamilnadu (background); first south-west monsoon clouds are striking the Western Ghats.
8. South-west monsoon rains at Kovalam.
9. Sastha or Ayyappa temple in monsoon rains; Poonjar on the Menacil river.
10. Malayalis praying at the Vaikam Temple.
11. Sacred room in a Malabar Nair home; ceremonial swords on rack (top); brass oil lamp (foreground); and (left) a kindi, a vessel for holding and pouring water.
12. Stone dancing figure in ceremonial and shrine hall, Padmanabhapuram Palace.
13. Fishermen setting out to sea, Tellicherry.
14. Fishermen hauling nylon nets, near Alleppey.
15. Weekly market, south of Trivandrum.
16. Mappila (Malabar Muslim) fishermen, Cannanore beach.
17. Muslim family on Kovalam beach.
18. The spice warehouse, Jew Town, Cochin. The Jews came early to Kerala, probably in AD 70, though legends speak of King Solomon's ships trading with the Malabar Coast.
19. Roadside garage, Malabar.
20. Coir trading activity, Alleppey.
21. Man changing truck tyres at a petrol pump; the poster advocates family planning; south of Trivandrum.
22. Schoolgirls at a Trivandrum bus stop; the memorial is to A. K. Gopalan of the Communist Party of India (Marxist); the Malayalam writing reads: 'If not today, then tomorrow.'
23. Traffic, pedestrians and shoppers below commercial hoardings, Trichur.
24. Country-craft transporting coconut products from villages to Alleppey warehouses lining a canal.
25. Guardian at the Kollengode Palace.
26. Writer and Ezhava leader Murkot Kumaran's oil portrait in his son's house, Tellicherry.
27. Namboodiri bride and relatives during a premarital ritual, Trichur.
28. Syrian Christian lady with cat and oil portrait of her grandmother, near Palai.
29. Muslim (Mappila) trading family at midday rest, New Mahe.
30. Young boy in a Malappuram home.
31. College girls and woman with baby at a bus stop; the store sells bathroom fittings; Trivandrum.
32. Man and boy in front of a shop-shutter advertisement for tea, Calicut.
33. Red car and bus, near Trichur.
34. Children's playground, Calicut.
35. Farmer pushing a Japanese tractor to his paddy field, Kuttanad, south of Kottayam.
36. Repairing a ceiling fan in a coir factory, Alleppey.
37. Vikram Sarabhai Space Centre exhibition stall, Varkala.
38. Farmer drying paddy alongside a canal, Kuttanad.
39. Paddy fields being ploughed in southern Kerala.
40. Padanaickan tribesman with a transistor radio, Nilambur forest.
41. Tribal women and children at a tea shop, next to a photographer's backdrop; Attapadi.
42. Cholanaickan tribesman with bamboo tubes full of honey for bartering at a shop, Nilambur forest.
43. Cholanaickan woman with children and parrots, Nilambur forest.

44 Parrots and cooking utensils on a platform; Cholanaickan man in lower background; Nilambur forest.

45 Onam festival snake-boat pageant, Aranmulla, on the Pampa river.

46 Bird-head prow of temple boat honouring Garuda, the vehicle of Vishnu; Onam festival, Aranmulla.

47 Gathering at Guruvayur Temple.

48 Trichur Pooram festival on the Vadukkanathan Temple grounds.

49 Make-up for a Bhagwati (Mother Goddess) Teyyam (literally 'God's Dance'), Malabar.

50 Dressing up for a Teyyam near Badagara.

51 Sarpam Thullal (snake worship), Alleppey district.

52 Worshipper being blessed during a Muchilot Bhagwati Teyyam, Malabar.

53 Kalamandalam students exercising in a Kathakali theatre class; (background) others beating maddalam and chenda drums, Cheruthurthy.

54 A Kalamandalam Kathakali guru teaching students the gesture for dripping honey or nectar.

55 Players about to begin a Kathakali play, Trivandrum.

56 The noted Kathakali actor Kalamandalam Krishnan Nair being made up, Ettumanur.

57 The Valliamma, a Namboodiri priestess, at the snake temple, Manarsala.

58 Musicians with their instruments (left to right): a mridangam, a veena, a tampura and a violin. The mural shows Durga, the Mother Goddess, and attendants; Navrati festival, Swati Tirunal Palace, Trivandrum.

59 Gurukkul Govindankutty Nair (left) and his son Sathyanarayan, demonstrating to students the South Indian martial art, Kalaripayattu; Trivandrum.

60 Patient being massaged at the Arya Vaidya Sala (hospital), Kottakal, where India's ancient system of medicine is practised.

61 Women peeling cashews in a Calicut factory.

62 Textile factory in Calicut.

63 Women workers sifting black pepper in Mattancharry.

64 Tamil worker in a Western Ghats plantation carrying a bucket of cardamom.

65 May Day Communist tableau, Cochin, re-enacting the Punnapra Vayalar shooting during a Communist-led worker's uprising against the Maharaja of Travancore's government in 1946. The poster demands: '8 hours work only.'

66 Decorative plaques with portraits of Lenin being sold on May Day, Calicut.

67 Hanuman the Hindu God and the Marxist party symbol painted on the wall of a Malabar hut; in the background, man collecting coconuts.

68 Women sifting paddy at Olappamana, a traditional Namboodiri illam or mansion in Palghat district.

69 Chaldean Church, Trichur. This Syrian Christian sect dates back to the arrival of Cana Thomas and a group of 400 East Syrian families, in AD 345, at Cranganore.

70 Kuttichira Mosque, Calicut.

71 The British-built former Residency – now a government guest house – where the Resident or Viceroy's representative lived in Quilon during the Raj.

72 Bullock and cart, Kollengode. Western Ghats in background.

73 Mappila schoolgirls returning from school, Tirurangadi.

74 Mappila boys walking the ramparts of Bekal Fort, built by the Kaladi Nayakas (1500-1763), the Karnataka kings.

75 Malayali civil servant (back to the camera) entertaining a visitor, Fort Cochin. The Chinese nets suggest the ancient trade with China.

76 Interior of the Jewish Synagogue, Mattancherry, Cochin; originally built in the 16th century. The present structure dates from the 18th century.

77 Employees of Kottayam's Malayalam Manorama lining up for Christmas presents from the Syrian Christian proprietors.

78 The Catholicos, Mar Baselios Marthoma Mathews I, the head of the Malankara Syrian Orthodox Church (seated), flanked

by Metropolitans, awaits the arrival of Pope John Paul II to the Mar Elia Cathedral, Kottayam, in February 1986.

79 *Syrian Christian Metropolitan holding a cross for a bride to kiss during her marriage ceremony in Kottayam.*

80 *Two Syrian Christian priests of St Mary's Church, Niranam, Kottayam district, at a lunch on the anniversary of a funeral.*

81 *Camel and sheep at a circus, Trivandrum.*

82 *The Parassinikkadavu Snake Park, near Cannanore.*

83 *Repaired boat being delivered by bullock cart, near Kovalam.*

84 **Kalapoolttu**, *a levelling with bullocks competition, Quilon district.*

85 *Wild elephants swimming from island to island, Periyar Wildlife Preserve.*

86 *Graffiti on a Periyar boat.*

87 *Swimming pool, Ashok Hotel, Kovalam.*

4

11

12

13

14

19

20

23

24

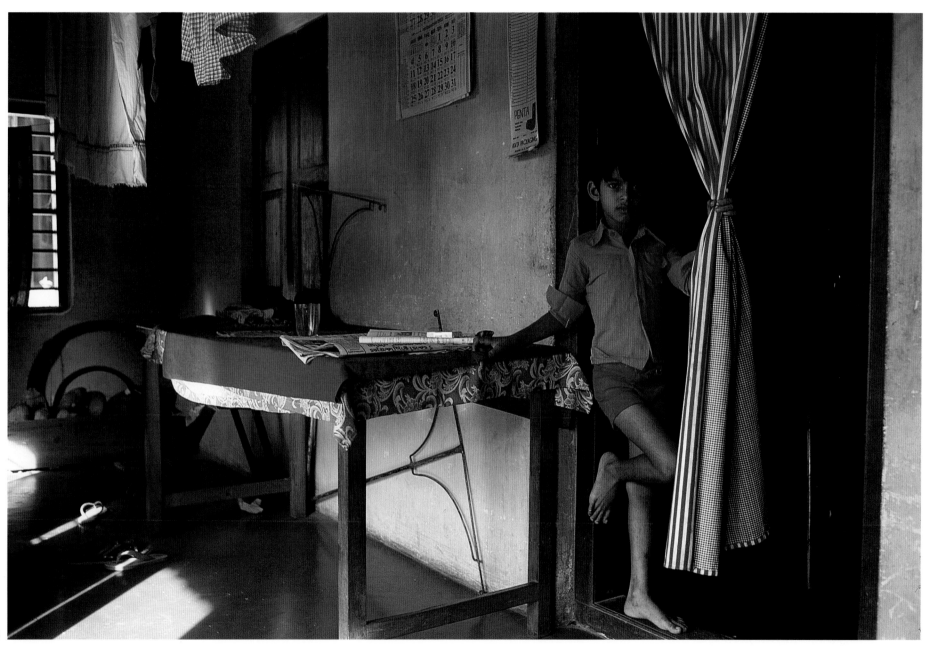

36

37

44

48

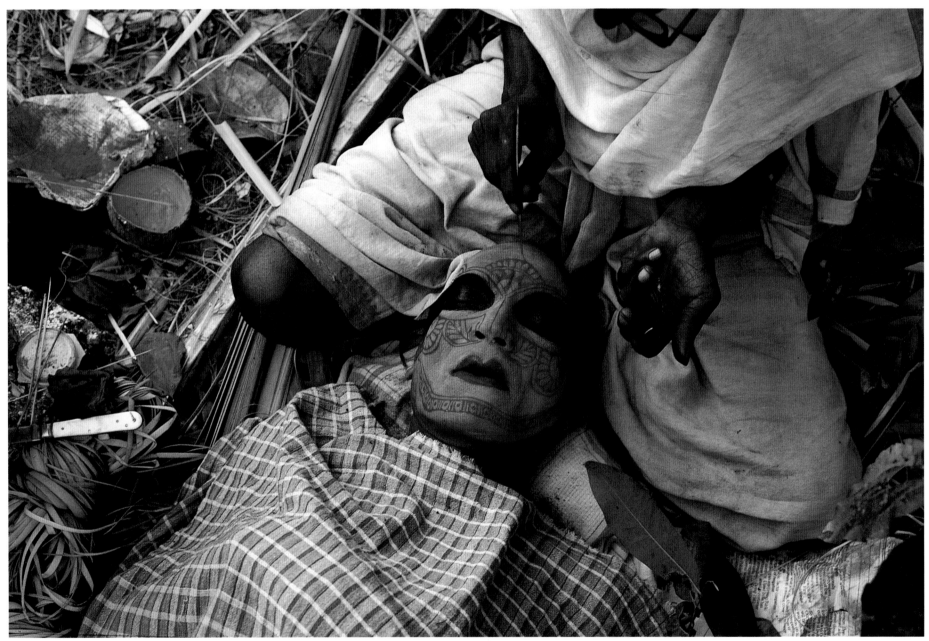

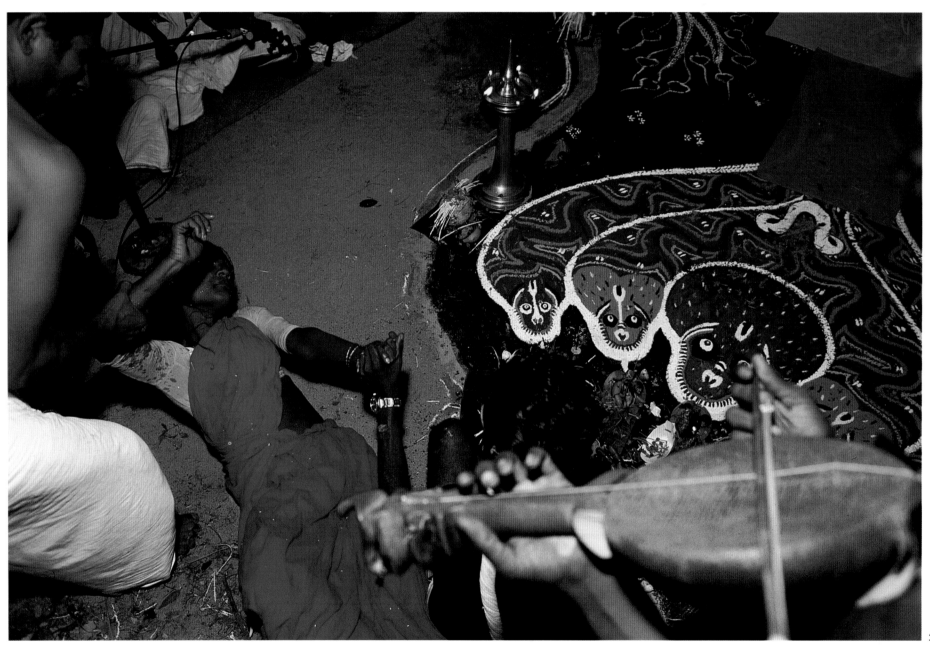

58

66

69

70